Contents

Pumpkin Muffins

Ingredients:

- 1 large onion, chopped
- 3/4 cup yellow cornmeal
- 1 tsp baking powder
- ½ tsp baking soda
- ½ tsp pumpkin pie spice
- ¼ tsp sal t
- 2 eggs, beaten
- 1 can pumpkin puree
- ½ cup dark brown sugar
- ¼ cup pure canola oil
- 1 cup chopped pecans (optional)

Directions:

1. Grease muffin cups or line with regular or small paper muffin liners. In a large bowl, stir flour, cornmeal, baking powder, baking soda, and salt and make a well in the center. In a small bowl, stir together the eggs, pumpkin, sugar, and oil. Make a well in the center of the dry **Ingredients** and pour in the egg mixture. Stir just barely blended and then fold in pecans. Divide the batter evenly among prepared muffin tin cups. Bake at 425°F in preheated oven for 15 to 20 minutes or until done. If you insert a toothpick into center of a muffin and it comes out clean, the muffins are done. These muffins go great with the Pumpkin Bisque recipe.

Pumpkin Corn Bread

Ingredients (makes 12 servings or double for 24):

- 6 tbsp. butter, melted
- 2 cups cornmeal
- 1/3 cup sugar
- 2 tbsp. corn flour
- 2 tsp baking powder
- 1 tsp baking soda
- 1 tsp salt
- 1/4 teaspoon pumpkin pie spic e
- 1 cup buttermilk
- 8 oz. sour cream (nonfat or low fat)
- 1 egg, lightly beaten
- 3/4 cup canned pumpkin

- Butter (optional)

Directions:

1. Preheat oven to 350◦F. Coat 12-inch cast-iron skillet with 2 tablespoons of the butter; set aside remaining butter.
2. In a large mixing bowl combine cornmeal, sugar, corn flour, baking powder, baking soda, salt, and pumpkin pie spice. In another bowl combine remaining butter, buttermilk, sour cream, egg, and pumpkin; whisk into cornmeal mixture. Pour into prepared skillet. To make muffins instead of cornbread slices, use muffin pans and cupcake liners. Bake 8-10 minutes or until done. Serves 12-24 depending on whether you make mini-muffins or full-size muffins.
3. Bake for 20 to 25 minutes or until a toothpick comes out clean. Cool on wire rack; serve warm with whipped butter .
4. TIP: Prepare and bake as directed. Wrap cooled corn bread in foil inside plastic containers. Store in refrigerator up to 2 days. Reheat on 325◦F, still wrapped in foil (or 300◦F for muffins) for 10-15 minutes until warm. You can serve one wrapped muffin or two mini muffins with a packet of honey butter.

Monster Meatloaf & Potato Cupcakes

Ingredients

- (Makes 12 servings; double this recipe to get 24 meat cupcakes):
- 2 baking potatoes, peeled and quartered
- 1 1/4 pounds sweet or hot Italian sausage, casings removed (or whatever meat you like, such as hamburger or turkey beef)
- 1 onion, finely chopped
- 1 yellow bell pepper, finely chopped
- 1/2 cup heavy cream
- 2 tablespoons butte r
- salt
- 1 1/4 cups breadcrumbs
- 2 large eggs, beaten

Directions:

1. Preheat the oven to 400 degrees Line a 12-cup muffin pan with foil cupcake liners (paper liners will not be sturdy enough). In a medium saucepan, bring the potatoes to a boil in salted water. Cook until tender, about 15 minutes; drain. While potatoes are boiling, cook the sausage or whatever meat you prefer over medium-high heat for about 5 – 10 minutes. Drain grease and add the onion and bell pepper.
2. Cook for about five minute until onion and pepper are soft. Using an electric mixer, beat the potatoes, cream, butter and 1/2 teaspoon salt until smooth. Using your hands, combine the breadcrumbs and sausage mixture, breaking up any large pieces. Mix in the eggs; season with

1/2 teaspoon salt. Fill each prepared muffin cup with 1/3 cup sausage mixture. Bake until browned, about 30 minutes. Let cool and transfer to a party platter.

3. Fill a pastry bag fitted with a star tip (or you can use a plastic food storage bag with a corner cut off) with the mashed potatoes and pipe onto each cupcake .
4. TIP: This is more labor intensive than other appetizers but like a couple of the dessert options, I think it is worth the effort. These are so filling and unusual and I like that they are single serve portions. I always get lots of raves from the guys and recipe requests from female guests. Be sure to place a homemade sign next to the plate to identify these cool "Monster Meat and Potato Cupcakes." You may want to include this request "One Per Guest Please!"

Halloween Sangria

Ingredients:

- 1 grapefruit, peeled and cut into supreme style segments
- 2 oranges, peeled and cut into supreme style segments
- 1 blood orange, cut into slices
- 2 clementine mandarins, cut into slice s
- 10 kumquats cut into slices
- 2 tablespoons honey
- ½ cup orange liqueur like Grand Marnier
- 2 cups chilled sparkling water
- juice of 1 lemon
- bottle of chilled Moscato wine (or wine of preference)
- Note: For non-alcoholic version, substitute sparkling white grape juice for wine and liqueur
- Ice

Directions:

1. Put the citrus fruit slices and segments in a pitcher. Add the honey and orange liqueur, let macerate for at least 30 minutes.
2. Add the chilled sparkling water, Moscato wine, lemon juice and ice. Mix well. The citrus Moscato sangria can be served immediately or keep refrigerated 'til serve.
3. TIP: When serving the sangria use a spoon or fork to put some of the citrus pieces into each glass. Also, you can buy ready-made Sangria (white or red) instead of buying all these

Vampire Punch

Ingredients:

- 45 – 50 oz. Red Fruit Punch
- 6oz. Frozen Lemonade concentrate
- 6 oz. Frozen Grape Juice concentrate

- 3 cups Lemon Lime Soda
- 6 cups water
- 4 small oranges (washed and sliced)
- 1 small jar cherrie s

Directions:

1. Thaw lemonade and grape juice before making punch (30 – 40 minutes should be enough time). Put punch, lemonade, grape juice, and water into large punch bowl. Just before serving, add lemon lime soda and fruit and/or fake hand or fake bugs (sanitize first).

Mad Scientist Punch

Ingredients:

- 3 cans (12 oz. each) frozen pineapple-orange juice
- concentrate, thawed
- 2 cups water
- 1 envelope unsweetened orange Kool-Aid mix
- 2 liters lemon-lime soda, chilled
- 1 pint orange sherbet, softene d

Directions:

1. In a punch bowl, combine the juice concentrate, water and Kool-Aid mix; stir in soda. Top with scoops of sherbet. Serve immediately in plastic disposable cups or buy mini plastic beakers in the dollar store and they are also available on Amazon by the dozen.

Pumpkin Milk Shakes

Ingredients:

- 1 cup orange juice
- cups vanilla ice cream
- 1 cup canned pumpkin
- 1/2 cup packed brown sugar
- 1 teaspoon ground cinnamo n
- 1/2 teaspoon ground ginger
- 1/2 teaspoon ground nutmeg
- Black or red licorice twists (optional)

Directions:

1. Put the first seven **Ingredients** in a blender. Cover and blend until smooth. Serve immediately with licorice stirrers, if desired.

Hot Apple Cider

Ingredients:

- 2 quarts or liters apple juice
- 1 cup orange juice
- 1/2 cup lemon juice
- 1/2 cup brown sugar
- 1-2 cinnamon sticks
- 1 tbsp. whole cloves in spice ba g

Directions:

1. Heat apple juice almost to boiling. Add spice bag and cinnamon sticks. Simmer 5-10 minutes. Add orange juice, lemon juice and brown sugar. Heat and serve. Makes approximately 20 (4 oz.) servings.
2. TIP: Keep warm in a coffee carafe or thermos. Place sign next to carafe so no one mistakes it for coffee. Make sure you have Styrofoam cups next to thermos or carafe. Or you can have ready for guests if you buy lids for your cups. Just be sure to label cups so guests know what they are consuming.

Creamy Cocoa

Ingredients:

- 14 oz. sweet condensed milk
- ½ cup unsweetened cocoa
- 1/8 tsp salt
- 1 ½ tsp vanilla extract
- 6 cups hot water
- Mini marshmallows (optional)

Directions:

1. In 2-quart glass container, combine all **Ingredients** except marshmallows. Microwave on HIGH 8 to 10 minutes. Stop after four minutes and stir and then resume heating. Top with marshmallows (sometimes around the holidays you can find colored marshmallows; I stock up seasonally).
2. TIP: This cocoa mix can be stored in refrigerator up to 5 days. Mix well and reheat before serving.

Pumpkin & Peanut Butter Treats

Ingredients:

- 2½ cups wheat flour
- 2 eggs
- 1/2 cup canned pumpkin
- 2 tbsp peanut butter
- ½ tsp salt

- ½ tsp cinnamo n

Directions:

1. Preheat oven to 350◦F. Whisk together the flour, eggs, pumpkin, peanut butter, salt, and cinnamon in a bowl. Add water as needed to help make the dough workable, but the dough should be dry and stiff. Roll the dough into a 1/2-inch-thick roll. Cut into 1/2-inch pieces. Bake in preheated oven until hard, about 40 minutes.
2. TIP: You can use Halloween cookie cutters or bone cookie cutters if you have them.

No Bake Pumpkin Dog Treats

Ingredients:

- 1 cup canned pumpkin
- ½ cup peanut butter
- ¼ cups rolled oats
- 1 tsp cinnamon
- ¼ cup hone y

Directions:

1. Mix all Ingredients in bowl and roll into 1-inch balls. Place on parchment paper and refrigerate for one hour. Store in Tupperware and will last for one week.

Apple Crunch Pup Cakes

Ingredients:

- 3 cups water
- ½ tsp vanilla extract
- 1 egg
- tbsp honey
- ¼ cups unsweetened/natural applesauce
- 1 tbsp baking powder
- 4 cups wheat flour
- 1 apple, diced or choppe d

2. TIP: You can add Halloween sprinkles to the balls before the chocolate hardens. I buy a variety pack (available in most grocery stores) so I can use different sprinkles to create different effects.

Severed Toe Treats

Ingredients:

- Refrigerated ready-made crescent rolls
- Mustard

- Hot dogs
- Ketchup (optional)

Directions:

1. Cut hot dogs in half and roll half inside a crescent roll that has been lightly coated with mustard and shaped to resemble a toe. Be sure to leave the hot dog sticking out on one end to be the "severed toe."
1. When done cooking, add a bit of mustard to create a big toenail. You can add a drizzle of ketchup around the "toenail" to enhance the severed effect. These can be served as is or with ketchup dipping sauce.

Monster Meatballs

Ingredients:

- 1 jar of grape jelly
- 1 bottle Heinz Chili Sauce
- One Package of Frozen Meatballs or make your own

Directions:

1. Mix all Ingredients and then cook in Crockpot for 6 hours. Simmer on lowest heat during party and stir periodically .
1. TIP: You can get frozen meatballs fairly cheap in the freezer aisle of grocery story or you can also make your own by buying a large container of ground beef on sale (it's always on sale) and then rolling the meat into small balls and brown in a frying pan on medium heat. You don't need to season the meat since you'll be adding chili sauce and jelly for flavoring. Remember to make the meatballs small (about 1") so they go farther.

Monster Claws

Ingredients:

- 4 small boneless skinless chicken breasts (1 lb.), cut lengthwise in half (as pictured)
- 1 pkt. Extra Crispy Seasoned Coating Mix (I like Kraft Shake 'N Bake Original Mix)
- ¼ red pepper, cut into 8 triangular pieces
- ½ cup teriyaki or barbecue sauce

Directions:

1. Roll chicken in coating mix as directed on package. Place on baking sheet sprayed with cooking spray.
2. Bake at 400ºF for 15 min. or until chicken is done .
3. Make a 1/2-inch slit in the thinner end of each chicken strip; insert a red pepper triangle in slit for the monster's claw.
4. Serve with your favorite homemade dipping sauce or store bought teriyaki or barbecue sauce.

TIP: You can substitute fried cheese sticks for chicken fingers or serve both. Follow the same Directions for creating the claw. Also, you can put two monster claws in a baggie and seal for easy, hygienic serving. Just be sure to label if you serve both fried cheese and chicken. Halloween decals (available at dollar stores) can be affixed to the baggies along with the name of the recipe to create a more pleasing effect.

Ghoulish Goulash

Ingredients:

- 1 pounds lean ground beef
- 1 medium onion, chopped
- 1 can diced tomatoes
- 1 small bag frozen whole kernel corn
- 2 cups uncooked macaroni
- 1 can beef broth
- 3 tablespoons chili seasoning
- 1 tablespoon sugar
- 1 teaspoon garlic
- 1 teaspoon dried oregano
- 1 teaspoon salt
- 1/2 teaspoon black pepper
- 1 cup shredded cheddar cheese (optional)
- 1 cup sour cream (optional)

Directions:

1. In a large skillet, brown the ground beef and onion.
2. Add the remaining Ingredients, except cheese, to the skillet and mix well.
3. Immediately pour mixture into crock pot and cook for 3 1/2 hours on low.
4. When the goulash is nearly done, turn to lowest heat and put out with label identifying dish. This is a great party dish because it is very filling. I place Dixie cups next to it rather than bowls or you can serve already in the cups with shredded cheddar cheese sprinkled on top; cover with plastic wrap and add a “Ghoulish Goulash” label over the plastic wrap; it tastes good room temperature) and it is something that you don’t often see served at parties so guests will appreciate it.

Pumpkin Bisque

Ingredients:

- 1 large onion, chopped
- 2 cloves garlic, chopped
- 1 tablespoon butter or margarine
- 1 16-ounce can pumpkin puree

- 4 cups chicken stock
- 1/2 teaspoon freshly ground black pepper
- 1/4 teaspoon ground allspice
- 1/2 teaspoon sugar
- 1 cup half-and-half or light cream
- 1/4 cup dry sherry
- grated nutmeg

Directions:

1. Sauté the onion and garlic in the butter until they are soft. Add the pumpkin, chicken stock, ground pepper, allspice, sugar, and sherry. Bring to a boil and cover. Simmer the soup for 30 minutes. Place the mixture in a blender and puree until smooth. Return the soup to the pot, add the half-and-half, and simmer until well heated. Garnish with the nutmeg and serve.
2. This soup can be served either hot or cold and can be served in single servings. It goes great with pumpkin cornbread or pumpkin muffins or mini pumpkin muffins (see next recipe) that can be individually wrapped and served.

Pumpkin Muffins

These go good with Pumpkin Bisque.

Ingredients:

- 1 large onion, chopped
- 3/4 cup yellow cornmeal
- 1 tsp baking powder
- ½ tsp baking soda
- ½ tsp pumpkin pie spice
- ¼ tsp sal t
- 2 eggs, beaten
- 1 can pumpkin puree
- ½ cup dark brown sugar
- ¼ cup pure canola oil
- 1 cup chopped pecans (optional)

Directions:

1. Grease muffin cups or line with regular or small paper muffin liners. In a large bowl, stir flour, cornmeal, baking powder, baking soda, and salt and make a well in the center. In a small bowl, stir together the eggs, pumpkin, sugar, and oil. Make a well in the center of the dry Ingredients and pour in the egg mixture. Stir just barely blended and then fold in pecans. Divide the batter evenly among prepared muffin tin cups. Bake at 425°F in preheated oven for 15 to 20 minutes or until done. If you insert a toothpick into center of a muffin and it comes out clean, the muffins are done. These muffins go great with the Pumpkin Bisque recipe.

Pumpkin Corn Bread

Ingredients (makes 12 servings or double for 24):

- 6 tbsp. butter, melted
- 2 cups cornmeal
- 1/3 cup sugar
- 2 tbsp. corn flour
- 2 tsp baking powder
- 1 tsp baking soda
- 1 tsp salt
- 1/4 teaspoon pumpkin pie spic e
- 1 cup buttermilk
- 8 oz. sour cream (nonfat or low fat)
- 1 egg, lightly beaten
- 3/4 cup canned pumpkin
- Butter (optional)

Directions:

1. Preheat oven to 350◦F. Coat 12-inch cast-iron skillet with 2 tablespoons of the butter; set aside remaining butter.
2. In a large mixing bowl combine cornmeal, sugar, corn flour, baking powder, baking soda, salt, and pumpkin pie spice. In another bowl combine remaining butter, buttermilk, sour cream, egg, and pumpkin; whisk into cornmeal mixture. Pour into prepared skillet. To make muffins instead of cornbread slices, use muffin pans and cupcake liners. Bake 8-10 minutes or until done. Serves 12-24 depending on whether you make mini-muffins or full-size muffins.
3. Bake for 20 to 25 minutes or until a toothpick comes out clean. Cool on wire rack; serve warm with whipped butter .
4. TIP: Prepare and bake as directed. Wrap cooled corn bread in foil inside plastic containers. Store in refrigerator up to 2 days. Reheat on 325◦F, still wrapped in foil (or 300◦F for muffins) for 10-15 minutes until warm. You can serve one wrapped muffin or two mini muffins with a packet of honey butter.

Monster Meatloaf & Potato Cupcakes

Ingredients

- (Makes 12 servings; double this recipe to get 24 meat cupcakes):
- 2 baking potatoes, peeled and quartered
- 1 1/4 pounds sweet or hot Italian sausage, casings removed (or whatever meat you like, such as hamburger or turkey beef)
- 1 onion, finely chopped

- 1 yellow bell pepper, finely chopped
- 1/2 cup heavy cream
- 2 tablespoons butte r
- salt
- 1 1/4 cups breadcrumbs
- 2 large eggs, beaten

Directions:

1. Preheat the oven to 400 degrees Line a 12-cup muffin pan with foil cupcake liners (paper liners will not be sturdy enough). In a medium saucepan, bring the potatoes to a boil in salted water. Cook until tender, about 15 minutes; drain. While potatoes are boiling, cook the sausage or whatever meat you prefer over medium-high heat for about 5 – 10 minutes. Drain grease and add the onion and bell pepper.
2. Cook for about five minute until onion and pepper are soft. Using an electric mixer, beat the potatoes, cream, butter and 1/2 teaspoon salt until smooth. Using your hands, combine the breadcrumbs and sausage mixture, breaking up any large pieces. Mix in the eggs; season with 1/2 teaspoon salt. Fill each prepared muffin cup with 1/3 cup sausage mixture. Bake until browned, about 30 minutes. Let cool and transfer to a party platter.
3. Fill a pastry bag fitted with a star tip (or you can use a plastic food storage bag with a corner cut off) with the mashed potatoes and pipe onto each cupcake .
4. TIP: This is more labor intensive than other appetizers but like a couple of the dessert options, I think it is worth the effort. These are so filling and unusual and I like that they are single serve portions. I always get lots of raves from the guys and recipe requests from female guests. Be sure to place a homemade sign next to the plate to identify these cool "Monster Meat and Potato Cupcakes." You may want to include this request "One Per Guest Please!"

Halloween Sangria

Ingredients:

- 1 grapefruit, peeled and cut into supreme style segments
- 2 oranges, peeled and cut into supreme style segments
- 1 blood orange, cut into slices
- 2 clementine mandarins, cut into slice s
- 10 kumquats cut into slices
- 2 tablespoons honey
- ½ cup orange liqueur like Grand Marnier
- 2 cups chilled sparkling water
- juice of 1 lemon
- bottle of chilled Moscato wine (or wine of preference)
- Note: For non-alcoholic version, substitute sparkling white grape juice for wine and liqueur

- Ice

Directions:

1. Put the citrus fruit slices and segments in a pitcher. Add the honey and orange liqueur, let macerate for at least 30 minutes.
2. Add the chilled sparkling water, Moscato wine, lemon juice and ice. Mix well. The citrus Moscato sangria can be served immediately or keep refrigerated 'til serve.
3. TIP: When serving the sangria use a spoon or fork to put some of the citrus pieces into each glass. Also, you can buy ready-made Sangria (white or red) instead of buying all these

Vampire Punch

Ingredients:

- 45 – 50 oz. Red Fruit Punch
- 6oz. Frozen Lemonade concentrate
- 6 oz. Frozen Grape Juice concentrate
- 3 cups Lemon Lime Soda
- 6 cups water
- 4 small oranges (washed and sliced)
- 1 small jar cherrie s

Directions:

1. Thaw lemonade and grape juice before making punch (30 – 40 minutes should be enough time). Put punch, lemonade, grape juice, and water into large punch bowl. Just before serving, add lemon lime soda and fruit and/or fake hand or fake bugs (sanitize first).

Mad Scientist Punch

Ingredients:

- 3 cans (12 oz. each) frozen pineapple-orange juice
- concentrate, thawed
- 2 cups water
- 1 envelope unsweetened orange Kool-Aid mix
- 2 liters lemon-lime soda, chilled
- 1 pint orange sherbet, softene d

Directions:

1. In a punch bowl, combine the juice concentrate, water and Kool-Aid mix; stir in soda. Top with scoops of sherbet. Serve immediately in plastic disposable cups or buy mini plastic beakers in the dollar store and they are also available on Amazon by the dozen.

Pumpkin Milk Shakes

Ingredients:

- 1 cup orange juice
- cups vanilla ice cream
- 1 cup canned pumpkin
- 1/2 cup packed brown sugar
- 1 teaspoon ground cinnamo n
- 1/2 teaspoon ground ginger
- 1/2 teaspoon ground nutmeg
- Black or red licorice twists (optional)

Directions:

1. Put the first seven Ingredients in a blender. Cover and blend until smooth. Serve immediately with licorice stirrers, if desired.

Hot Apple Cider

Ingredients:

- 2 quarts or liters apple juice
- 1 cup orange juice
- 1/2 cup lemon juice
- 1/2 cup brown sugar
- 1-2 cinnamon sticks
- 1 tbsp. whole cloves in spice ba g

Directions:

1. Heat apple juice almost to boiling. Add spice bag and cinnamon sticks. Simmer 5-10 minutes. Add orange juice, lemon juice and brown sugar. Heat and serve. Makes approximately 20 (4 oz.) servings.
2. TIP: Keep warm in a coffee carafe or thermos. Place sign next to carafe so no one mistakes it for coffee. Make sure you have Styrofoam cups next to thermos or carafe. Or you can have ready for guests if you buy lids for your cups. Just be sure to label cups so guests know what they are consuming.

Creamy Cocoa

Ingredients:

- 14 oz. sweet condensed milk
- ½ cup unsweetened cocoa
- 1/8 tsp salt
- 1 ½ tsp vanilla extract
- 6 cups hot water
- Mini marshmallows (optional)

Directions:

1. In 2-quart glass container, combine all Ingredients except marshmallows. Microwave on HIGH 8 to 10 minutes. Stop after four minutes and stir and then resume heating. Top with marshmallows (sometimes around the holidays you can find colored marshmallows; I stock up seasonally).
2. TIP: This cocoa mix can be stored in refrigerator up to 5 days. Mix well and reheat before serving.

Pumpkin & Peanut Butter Treats

Ingredients:

- 2½ cups wheat flour
- 2 eggs
- 1/2 cup canned pumpkin
- 2 tbsp peanut butter
- ½ tsp salt
- ½ tsp cinnamo n

Directions:

1. Preheat oven to 350∘F. Whisk together the flour, eggs, pumpkin, peanut butter, salt, and cinnamon in a bowl. Add water as needed to help make the dough workable, but the dough should be dry and stiff. Roll the dough into a 1/2-inch-thick roll. Cut into 1/2-inch pieces. Bake in preheated oven until hard, about 40 minutes.
2. TIP: You can use Halloween cookie cutters or bone cookie cutters if you have them.

No Bake Pumpkin Dog Treats

Ingredients:

- 1 cup canned pumpkin
- ½ cup peanut butter
- ¼ cups rolled oats
- 1 tsp cinnamon
- ¼ cup hone y

Directions:

1. Mix all Ingredients in bowl and roll into 1-inch balls. Place on parchment paper and refrigerate for one hour. Store in Tupperware and will last for one week.

Apple Crunch Pup Cakes

Ingredients:

- 3 cups water
- ½ tsp vanilla extract
- 1 egg

- tbsp honey
- ¼ cups unsweetened/natural applesauce
- 1 tbsp baking powder
- 4 cups wheat flour
- 1 apple, diced or choppe d

Kookie Cookies

(AKA 'Peanut Butter & Corn Chip No Bake Cookies')

Ingredients:

- 1 package (10 oz.) corn chips
- 1 cup light corn syrup
- 1 cup sugar
- 1 cup creamy peanut butter

Directions:

1. Spread corn chips in a greased 15 inch x 10 inch by 1 inch baking pan .
2. In a saucepan over medium heat, bring corn syrup and sugar to a boil, stirring frequently to help dissolve the sugar. Boil 1 minute.
3. Remove from heat; stir in peanut butter until smooth.
4. Pour mixture over corn chips.
5. Drizzle melted semi-sweet chocolate chips over the top.
6. Let cool and then tear gooey, yummy sweet into pieces. This may sound like a strange combination but the crunchy, salty corn chips are an excellent mix with the sweet **Ingredients** and peanut butter.

Candy Bar Dip Recipe

Ingredients:

- 1 (8-ounce) package cream cheese, softened
- ½ cup butter, softened
- 1 teaspoon vanilla
- 1 cup powdered sugar
- 2 tablespoons brown sugar
- 1 cup chocolate chips
- 1 cup coconut flake
- ½ cup slivered almond s

Directions:

1. Blend cream cheese and butter until smooth mixture.
2. Add in vanilla and sugars and beat until creamy.
3. Stir in chocolate chips, coconut and almonds.

4. Spoon into a serving bowl and top with more chocolate chips, coconut and almonds so it makes a pretty presentation.
5. Refrigerate until ready to serve.
6. Since this is pretty sweet, I like to serve with pretzel rods but graham crackers are good too.
7. Optional: Use food color to dye the cream cheese orange or green and/or add Halloween sprinkles on top.

Chocolate Chip Cookie Frankensteins

- (Makes 20; double recipe for 40 monster cookies)

Ingredients:

- 1 pkg (16oz.) chocolate chip cookie dough bar
- 1 1/2 cups powdered sugar
- 2 tablespoons water
- Green food colorin g
- 2/3 cup semi-sweet chocolate mini morsels plus extra to create monster "bolts"
- 40 White Chocolate Pieces or Morsels (for the eyes)
- Chocolate and orange sprinklesPrevent oven to 325° F. Grease and flour 40 mini-muffin cups. Cut dough into squares. Place one square into each cup.

Directions:

1. Bake for 10 to 13 minutes or until light golden brown. Cool for 10 minutes in pans on wire racks. Run knife around edge of cups; remove cups to wire racks to cool completely.
2. Melt 2/3 cup mini morsels in uncovered, microwave-safe bowl on HIGH power for 45 seconds or until completely melted and then stir. Spread melted chocolate on top of one cup; top with second cup. Press down slightly. Return to wire rack. Repeat with remaining cups for a total of 20. These are the heads. Let stand for 15 minutes or until set.
3. While waiting for that to cool, cut ends off of 40 white morsels to make flat for the eyes. To make pupils, dip toothpick into melted chocolate and make a small dots on bottoms of morsels.
4. Put a piece of wax paper under wire rack. Combine powdered sugar and water in small bowl. Add food coloring to desired green color. The glaze will be slightly thin, not spreadable like a frosting. Hold each head by seam and dip top cup into glaze. Return to wire rack to allow glaze to drip down over bottom cup. Repeat with others. Additional glaze can be spooned over the tops if needed. While glaze is still wet, sprinkle tops with sprinkles and press down lightly.
5. Take two morsel eyes and press onto glaze on top cup. For "bolts" use two mini morsels and lightly press onto side of bottom cup, using glaze for glue if needed.
6. TIP: Until the glaze is completely set, the eyes may slide, so watch carefully and just put back into place. Allow to set completely before attempting to move 'monsters'.

Pumpkin Cream Cheese Cupcakes

(Makes two dozen; double recipe to make four dozen cupcakes)

Ingredients :

- 3/4 cup butter, softened
- 2-1/2 cups sugar
- 3 eggs
- 1 can (15 ounces) pure pumpki n
- 2-1/3 cups all-purpose flour
- 1 tablespoon pumpkin pie spice
- 1 teaspoon baking powder
- 1 teaspoon ground cinnamon
- 3/4 teaspoon salt
- 1/2 teaspoon baking soda
- 1/2 teaspoon ground ginger
- 1 cup buttermilk

FROSTING:

- 1 package (8 ounces) cream cheese, softened
- 1/2 cup butter, softened
- 4 cups powdered sugar
- 1 teaspoon vanilla extract
- 2 teaspoons ground cinnamon

Directions:

1. Preheat oven to 350° .
2. In a large bowl, cream butter and sugar until light and fluffy.
3. Add eggs, one at a time, beating well after each addition. Add pumpkin.
4. Combine the flour, pie spice, baking powder, cinnamon, salt, baking soda, and ginger. Add to the creamed mixture while alternately adding the buttermilk, beating well after each addition.
5. Fill paper-lined muffin cups three-fourths full. Bake for 20-25 minutes or until a toothpick inserted in the center comes out clean.
6. Cool for 10 minutes before removing from pans to wire racks to cool completely.
7. **For frosting:** in a large bowl, beat cream cheese and butter until fluffy. Add powdered sugar, cinnamon, and vanilla; beat until smooth. Frost cupcakes. Insert plastic Halloween theme toppers in each cupcake (dollar store) or decorate with Halloween sprinkles.

Reese's Chocolate Chip Brownies

Ingredients :

- Chocolate Chip Cookie Dough Bar

- Large size peanut butter cups
- Brownie Mix

Directions:

1. Preheat oven to 350 degrees .

Make brownie mix according to Directions on the box.

2. Spray each hole with cooking spray. You can use any kind of pan that has wells, such as muffin tins.
3. Scoop big tablespoon of cookie dough & press into bottom of each square.
4. Top cookie dough with an upside down Reese's Peanut Butter Cup.
5. Fill the rest of the square with brownie mix.
6. Bake for 15 minutes. Remove & sprinkle w/Halloween sprinkles or can frost (or drizzle) w/ orange icing.

Mummy Cookie Balls

Ingredients (makes 48 mummies) :

- 1 pkg. (8 oz.) cream cheese, softened
- 36 OREO Cookies (whatever variety you prefer), crushed
- 3-1/2 pkg. (4 oz. each) White Chocolate (14 oz.)
- Chocolate sprinkles, miniature semi-sweet chocolate chips or whatever you want to use to decorate

Directions:

1. Mix cream cheese and cookie crumbs until blended.
2. Make into 1-inch balls. Freeze 10 min.
3. Melt 12 oz. white chocolate as directed on package .
4. Dip balls in melted chocolate; place in single layer on waxed paper-covered rimmed baking sheet. (Re-freeze balls if they become too soft to dip.) Refrigerate 1 hour or until firm.
5. Melt remaining chocolate as directed on package; spoon into small plastic bag and seal. Cut 1/8-inch piece from one bottom corner of bag. Squeeze bag to pipe chocolate onto each ball for the mummy's eyes; immediately add decorations for the eyeballs. Pipe remaining chocolate onto balls to resemble gauze strips. Refrigerate until firm. These can be made in advance and stored in refrigerator until the party.

Reese's Cupcakes

Ingredients :

- White or yellow cake mix
- Reese's Pieces

Directions:

1. Use any brand yellow or white cake mix (I like Pillsbury with pudding in the mix). Make

according to Directions and then add Reese's pieces. Pour batter into Halloween theme cupcake liners and bake.

2. Optional: Add chocolate or orange frosting, but they are so tasty and pretty that it's not necessary. So easy!

Candy Corn Pizza

Ingredients:

- 1 roll (16.5 oz.) refrigerated sugar cookies
- ½ cup creamy peanut butter
- 1 cup candy corn
- ½ cup raisins or craisins
- ¼ cup whipped white or vanilla ready-to-spread frosting (from can)

Directions:

1. Cover a 12-inch pizza pan with foil (be sure to use cooking spray on the foil). Cut cookie dough into 1/4-inch-thick slices and arrange in pan. With floured fingers, press slices so as to form a crust .
2. Bake at 350°F for 15 to 20 minutes or until golden brown. Cool completely. Carefully remove foil from crust and place crust on a serving platter or tray. Spread peanut butter (I like to use honey peanut butter but can be plain or even crunchy peanut butter) over crust. Sprinkle candy corn and raisins evenly over top. Or you can use other toppings as well or in place of, such as chocolate or butterscotch chips or slivered almonds. In small microwavable bowl, microwave frosting on High for no more than 10 to 15 seconds (should be thin so that you can drizzle it over cookie pizza). Wait five minutes and then cut into party-sized wedges or squares.
3. TIP: You can buy a giant premade cookie at most grocery store bakeries and simply add the toppings.

Harry Potter Chocolate Cauldrons

(Makes 12 cauldrons; double recipe to make two dozen)

Ingredients :

- 12 Devil's Food cupcakes
- Chocolate glaze (see below)
- Marshmallow filling (see below)
- 1/2 cup chocolate chips
- Edible gold glitter

Chocolate Glaze

- 6 ounces (1 cup) semi-sweet chocolate chips
- 4 tablespoons butte r

- In a double boiler, melt together the chocolate and butter, stirring until smooth. Glaze will be relatively thick. Remove from heat and let sit 5 minutes before use. If chocolate thickens too much, return to heat and stir until smooth and melted once more.

Marshmallow Filling

- 1 cup marshmallow fluff or cream
- 1/2 cup vegetable shortening
- 1/2 cup confectioners' sugar
- 2 teaspoons vanilla extract

Directions:

1. In a medium bowl, beat together the marshmallow fluff, shortening, sugar, and vanilla extract until light and fluffy, about 3-5 minutes.
2. Use a sharp knife to cut out a cavity in the bottom of the cupcake. When using a knife, I run it in a circular motion around the cupcake, while always pointing the knife towards the center (this will make the cavity cone shaped).
3. Dip the top of the cupcake into the chocolate glaze. Flip the cupcakes right side up and let rest until the chocolate sets, about 30 minutes. To speed up the process, place cupcakes in the refrigerator.
4. To make the cauldron feet, take 3 chocolate chips and form a small triangle, placing each chocolate chip roughly an inch from the others. Place the top of a cupcake onto the chocolate chips and push down ever so slightly so the chocolate chips will stick into the chocolate glaze. Repeat for the rest of the cupcakes.
5. Place remaining chocolate glaze into a piping bag and pipe a chocolate rim around the edge of the opening to the cauldron. If chocolate is too thick to pipe, heat chocolate glaze up until warm and allow to sit until glaze thickens slightly. If chocolate glaze is too runny to pipe, wait a few minutes until the glaze thickens to a pipe-able consistency. Alternatively, you could use a knife to spread the glaze around the edge of the cupcake.
6. Fill a pastry bag with marshmallow filling and pipe into the cavity of the cupcakes. Garnish the top with edible gold glitter or use plastic Halloween toppers.
7. To make cauldron handle, melt the remaining chocolate chips, stir until smooth, and place into a pastry bag. You don't need a special tip for this step; I simply cut off the very end of the pastry bag which was sufficient. On a non-stick mat or wax paper, pipe out the handles (feel free to use any pattern you'd like). I recommend measuring the cupcakes with a ruler to determine how wide you need to make the handles before piping. Let the chocolate set until hardened, approximately 30 minutes, before very carefully peeling off of the non-stick surface and placing into the top of each cupcake.

Pumpkin Whoopie Pies

Ingredients (makes 16 or double recipe to make 32):

- 1 pkg. (2-layer size) yellow cake mix

- 1 pkg. (3.4 oz.) vanilla flavor instant pudding
- 2 tsp. pumpkin pie spice
- 1 cup canned pumpkin
- 1/3 cup oil
- 1/3 cup water
- 3 eggs
- 1 pkg. (8 oz.) cream cheese, softened
- 1 jar (7 oz.) Marshmallow Crème or Fluf f
- ¼ tsp. ground cinnamon
- 1 tub (8 oz.) Whipped Topping, room temperature
- ½ cup Halloween sprinkles

Directions:

1. Beat first 7 Ingredients with mixer until well blended. Scoop into 32 mounds, 3 inches apart, on baking sheet sprayed with cooking spray, using about 2 tbsp. for each.
2. Bake at 350ºF 12 to 14 min. or until toothpick inserted in centers comes out clean. Cool on baking sheet for two minutes. Remove to wire racks; cool completely.
3. Beat cream cheese, marshmallow cream, ginger and cinnamon in large bowl with mixer until well blended. Whisk in COOL WHIP (whipped topping). Spread 3 Tbsp. onto flat side of 1 cake; top with second cake, flat-side down. Roll edge in sprinkles. Repeat with remaining cakes. Keep refrigerated.
4. TIP: You can dye the marshmallow cream orange instead of adding sprinkles or in addition to using sprinkles.

Swamp Cake

Ingredients :

- 1 pkg. devil's food cake mix
- 8 OREO Cookies, chopped
- 1 (8 oz.) tub of Whipped Topping, thawed
- 1-1/4 cups boiling water
- 2 pkg. (3 oz. each) Lime Flavor Gelatin
- 2 cups ice cubes
- 7 Soft & Chewy Candies
- 1 large Marshmallo w
- 5 worm-shaped chewy fruit snacks
- ½ tsp. black decorating gel
- 1 piece black licorice
- 1 Peanut Bar (1.6 oz.), cut into pieces
- 1 (1.2 oz.) Milk Chocolate bar with Nougat, cut into pieces

Directions:

1. Make cake batter and bake in 13x9-inch pan according to **Directions**. Once completely cooled, remove (inverted) from cake pan. Hollow out center of cake, leaving thin layer on bottom and about 2-inch-wide irregular-shaped border on sides. Crumble all the removed cake. Put aside 2 Tbsp. Mix remaining crumbled cake with chopped cookies.
2. Spread about 1/2 cup whipped topping onto bottom of hole in cake. Add boiling water to gelatin mixes in large bowl; stir 2 min. until completely dissolved. Add ice cubes; stir until gelatin starts to thicken. Stir in the 2 tbsp. cake crumbs you set aside. Spoon over whipped topping in cake. Add chewy candies as shown in photo. Refrigerate 3 hours or until gelatin is firm.
3. Frost sides and border of cake with remaining whipped topping. Press enough cookie crumb mixture into whipping topping to evenly cover whipped topping. Sprinkle remaining crumb mixture onto platter around cake .
4. Roll marshmallow into 3-inch-long piece; fold lengthwise in half and flatten slightly to resemble ghost. Place on cake; use decorating gel to make eyes. Decorate cake with remaining to resemble photo. Feel free to decorate according to whim, meaning you may add additional items (edible candy shaped like bones or tiny signs on toothpicks "Beware!" or "Warning!" or "R.I.P.!") or arrange differently.
5. Keep refrigerated until ready to serve.

Mini Pumpkin Pies

Ingredients (Makes 48 pies)

- 48 tart shells
- 1/3 cup granulated sugar
- 1/4 teaspoon salt
- 1 1/2 teaspoons pumpkin pie spice
- 1 cup pure pumpkin puree
- 1 teaspoon pure vanilla extract
- 1 5-ounce can evaporated milk 1 canister whipped cream

Directions:

1. In a medium bowl, mix on low speed: sugar, salt, pumpkin pie spice, egg, pumpkin, vanilla and evaporated milk. Beat until smooth.
2. Place mini tart shells on prepared baking sheet (lined with parchment paper). Using a small scooper, fill each mini tart shell with pumpkin pie filling.
3. Put pan into preheated 350°F oven and bake for 15-17 minutes or until shells are golden brown and the filling has set. Let cool and top with whipped cream and Halloween sprinkles or create a monster face on each pie by using chips and sprinkles.
4. TIP: These are for sale on Amazon if you have trouble finding the tart shells in your local grocery store.

Pumpkin Dump Cake

Ingredients:

- 4 eggs, beaten
- 2 cups cooked pumpkin
- 1 1/2 cups sugar
- 12 oz. can evaporated milk
- 1 teaspoon salt
- 1 teaspoon nutmeg
- 2 teaspoons cinnamon
- 1 yellow cake mix
- 1/2 cup chopped pecans (pecan halves)
- 2 sticks melted butte r

Directions:

1. Mix first 8 Ingredients together. Pour into a 13x9 inch pan. Sprinkle cake mix evenly over pumpkin mixture.
2. Sprinkle chopped or pecan halves over the cake mix, then pour melted butter evenly over the cake mix.
3. Bake at 350◦F for 45 – 60 minutes or until lightly browned. Serve plain or with whipped topping and Halloween sprinkles on top or you can add small plastic monster toppers that are available at most dollar store. I have also made simple signs attached to toothpicks, such as "Eat at your own risk!" and "R.I.P.!"

Pumpkin Fudge

Ingredients:

- 2 cups granulated sugar
- 1 cup packed light brown sugar
- 3/4 cup (1 1/2 sticks) butter
- 2/3 cup (5 oz. can) evaporated milk
- 1/2 cup pumpkin puree
- 2 teaspoons pumpkin pie spice
- 2 cups (12 ounce package) white chocolate chips
- 1 jar (7 oz.) marshmallow crème
- 1 cup chopped pecans (optional)
- 1 1/2 teaspoons vanilla extract candy thermometer

Directions:

1. Line a 13 x 9-inch baking pan with foil .
2. In a heavy medium saucepan, combine the sugar, brown sugar, evaporated milk, pumpkin,

butter and pumpkin pie spice. Bring to a full rolling boil over medium heat, stirring constantly for 10 to 12 minutes or until candy thermometer reaches 234° to 240° F (soft-ball stage).

3. Stir in white chocolate chips, marshmallow crème, nuts and vanilla extract and stir vigorously for 1 minute until chips are melted.
4. Immediately pour into prepared pan. Let stand on wire rack for 2 hours or until completely cooled. Refrigerate tightly cover
5. To cut, lift foil from pan. Remove foil and cut fudge into 1-inch pieces. Add dollar store spider web over the top or across the bottom of the plate to create spooky effect.
6. TIP: You can alter the recipe to make Chocolate Pumpkin Fudge or Peanut Butter Pumpkin Fudge to make this sweet treat even better! Swirl the pumpkin into the chocolate or peanut butter to create a colorful contrast.

Halloween Party Cake

Ingredients:

- 1 box white cake mix (I recommend Betty Crocker SuperMoist cake mix or Pillsbury cake mix with pudding
- 1 box chocolate cake mix (I recommend Betty Crocker SuperMoist or Pillsbury with pudding in mix)
- Black food coloring
- Purple food coloring
- Orange food coloring
- 12 oz. can white frosting (preferably whipped)

Directions:

Heat oven to 325°F. Grease a 12-cup tube cake pan with cooking spray. Make cakes according to box Directions. Divide the white cake into two separate bowls.

1. Add orange (red+yellow) food coloring to one bowl and mix to the desired color. Then, add purple (blue+red) to the other and mix to the desired color.
2. Pour 2/3 of the chocolate cake batter into a bowl and mix with a few drops of the black (blue, red & green) food coloring. Do not use all the batter or it won't fit in the pan. You may want to make cupcakes with the rest of the batter.
3. Pour 1/2 of the chocolate cake batter into the bottom of the greased pan. Slowly pour the purple over the top of the chocolate cake but do NOT stir it.
4. Next, pour the orange batter over the purple batter and pour in the rest of the chocolate batter. Bake as directed on box or until ready. Cool completely and remove from pan.

FROSTING:

Divide your frosting into 3 bowls: orange, purple and black. Microwave each bowl for a few seconds on high until it is smooth enough to drizzle over the cake .

5. Using a spoon, drizzle the black frosting back and forth around the whole ring in a striping

pattern until you use it all. Then do the same with the purple and then the orange.

6. Store loosely covered and unrefrigerated but out of the heat. Cake can be made up to two days in advance.

Easy Ice Cream

Ingredients:

- 24 Halloween theme cupcake liners (and spoons)
- 24-count muffin/cupcake pan(s)
- Chocolate ice cream
- Orange and lime swirl sherbet

Directions:

1. Ice cream is always a crowd pleaser but often requires too much time for a busy party supervisor. But here's a cool idea for a kids Halloween party that involves NO effort. Freeze individual scoops of chocolate and orange and/or lime sherbet in cupcake liners the night before the party. Remove from freezer and serve! Be sure to add a few festive Halloween sprinkles before putting ice cream "bowls" into freezer.
2. TIP: Drizzle chocolate syrup on top of each scoop and add Halloween sprinkles.

S'mores Bars

You don't even need a campfire to make these!
Ingredients :

- For the crust: 1 stick butter, room temperature
- 2/3 cup sugar
- 1 large egg
- 1 tsp vanilla extract
- 1/3 cup all-purpose flou r
- ¼ tsp salt
- 3 cups graham cracker crumbs

For the filling:

- 7 oz. marshmallow cream
- 1 cup miniature marshmallows
- 1 cup chocolate chips and/or chocolate candy pieces

Directions:

1. Preheat oven to 350°F. Grease a 9x13-inch baking pan with cooking spray.
2. Mix butter and sugar in large bowl. Beat 2-3 minutes until creamy. Add egg and vanilla on low speed. Fold in graham cracker crumbs, flour, and salt. Transfer 1/3 of the graham cracker mixture to a small bowl to go on top of the bars before baking. Press the remaining 2/3 of the graham mixture evenly into the prepared pan.

3. Spread the marshmallow cream over the crust. Sprinkle with chocolate chips or candies and place marshmallows on tip. Lastly, add the rest of the crust mixture. Bake until the marshmallows are golden-brown, about 15-20 minutes. Cool and cut into bars. So good!

Pumpkin Gingerbread

Ingredients:

- 3 cups sugar
- 1 cup canola oil
- 4 eggs
- 2/3 cup water
- 1 can (15 oz.) canned pumpkin
- 1 tsp ground cinnamon
- 2 tsp allspice
- 3 ½ cups all-purpose flour
- 2 tsp ground ginger
- 2 tsp baking soda
- ½ tsp baking powder
- 1 ½ tsp sal t

Directions:

1. Preheat oven to 350◦F. Grease two 9x5 inch loaf pans. In a large bowl, combine sugar, oil and eggs; beat until smooth. Add water and beat until well blended. Stir in pumpkin, ginger, allspice, and cinnamon.
2. In medium bowl, combine flour, soda, salt, and baking powder. Add dry **Ingredients** to pumpkin mixture and blend until all **Ingredients** are mixed. Divide batter between two prepared pans. Bake until toothpick comes out clean (50 minutes – one hour).
3. TIP: You can also make these as muffins or in mini-loaf pans for individual servings. If I make muffins I add orange cream cheese frosting, which is usually available in the fall but you can also use food dye to make your own using basic cream cheese frosting.

Halloween Crispy Treats

These are so retro they never go out of vogue! These sweet treats were first introduced in 1939.

Ingredients :

- ½ cup salted butter
- One bag (16 oz.) marshmallows or marshmallow crème
- 10 cups rice crispies cereal
- One bag (14 oz.) of candy corn or Halloween M & M'S
- Food coloring

Directions:

1. Melt butter and marshmallows (or marshmallow crème) together in the microwave until smooth.
2. In a large bowl combine cereal and candy coated chocolate pieces .
3. When the marshmallows are melted and smooth, add a couple drops of yellow and red food coloring (yellow+red=orange). Mix thoroughly. Pour marshmallow mixture onto cereal and candy. Stir until well mixed.
4. Pour into a buttered pan. With greased hands, press the mixture into the pan. Decorate the top with candy corns or Halloween M&Ms, as desired. Put in the refrigerator to set and then cut into squares.
5. TIP: You can shape into pumpkins creating a stem using pretzels and frosting. Don't add candy corn.

Sweet & Salty Roasted Pumpkin Seeds

(Makes 1 - 2 cups or double recipe)

Ingredients :

- 1 1/2 cup rinsed and cleaned whole pumpkin seeds
- 1 tablespoon olive oil
- 1/4 cup cinnamon sugar
- 2 teaspoon kosher salt

Directions:

1. Preheat oven to 400°.
2. Line a half sheet pan with parchment paper .
3. Add pumpkin seeds, drizzle with olive oil and sprinkle with cinnamon sugar and kosher salt.
4. Add seeds to oven and after ten minutes stir the nuts. Let the seeds cook for 7-8 minutes longer. Make sure to not let the sugar burn.
5. Pull the seeds out of the oven, sprinkle with a pinch more of kosher salt and let cool for 10 minutes.
6. After cool, break the seeds into smaller "chunks."

Creepy Eyeball (Deviled) Eggs

Ingredients:

- 6 hard-boiled eggs, peeled
- 3 tbsp mayonnaise or salad dressing
- ½ tsp ground mustard
- ¼ tsp salt & ¼ tsp pepper
- Paprika, if desired
- Red food color, if desired
- Green olives with pimento s

Directions:

1. Cut eggs lengthwise in half. Slip out yolks and mash with fork. Stir in mayonnaise, mustard, salt and pepper. Fill whites with egg yolk mixture, heaping it lightly. Sprinkle with paprika, if desired. Drizzle red food color to create bloodshot eyes, if desired. Cover and refrigerate up to 24 hours.
2. Note: You can make deviled eggs using this classic recipe or make using another recipe or buy ready-made in specialty store if pressed for time. Slice green olives keeping pimento face up to create eyeball. Add red food color to create "blood-shot" eyes (optional) or just sprinkle with paprika.

Pumpkin Pillows

Ingredients (makes 20 or double recipe for 40):

- 12 caramel cubes
- 1 tsp. water
- ½ cup regular or low fat sour cream
- 1 tsp. ground cinnamon
- 4 oz. cream cheese, softened
- ½ cup canned pumpkin
- 1 tbsp. brown sugar
- 1 tsp. flour
- ¼ tsp. orange zes t
- 20 won ton wrappers
- 1 egg white, lightly beaten
- 2 cups oil
- 1tbsp. powdered sugar

Directions:

1. Microwave caramels and water in medium microwaveable bowl on HIGH 30 sec.; stir until caramels are completely melted. Cool 2 min. Stir in sour cream and 1/2 tsp. cinnamon. Refrigerate until ready to use.
2. Beat cream cheese, pumpkin, brown sugar, flour, zest and remaining cinnamon until well blended. Spoon about 2 tsp. onto center of each won ton wrapper. Moisten edges with egg white; fold diagonally in half. Pinch edges together tightly to seal.
3. Heat oil in large saucepan on medium-high heat to 350ºF. Add won tons, in batches; cook 2 to 3 min. or until evenly browned. Drain. Cool slightly or to room temperature. Sprinkle with powdered sugar. Serve with caramel or chocolate sauce (sold in grocery stores on same aisle as ice cream cones and toppings).
4. Optional: Drizzle green or orange food color around the plate and/or place a little ghost in the middle of the plate.
5. TIP: Won ton wrappers dry out quickly so keep covered with damp towel. Can make and

refrigerate ahead of time. When time for party, place on baking sheet and bake for 10 – 15 minutes (or until thoroughly heated) at 350°F.

6. Wonton wrappers are thin sheets of flour and egg-based dough that are typically used to make wontons, dumplings, and egg rolls. The availability and in-store location of wonton wrappers vary by store, but they will almost always be in a refrigerated (or freezer) section.

Tasty Bones

Ingredients:

- 1 pkg. (11 oz.) refrigerated soft breadsticks
- ¼ cup grated Parmesan Cheese
- ½ cup ranch dressing
- 1 tbsp. hot pepper sauc e

Directions:

1. Heat oven to 375°F.
2. Cut breadsticks crosswise in half. Take a piece and stretch it until it is five inches. Tie a knot at each end.
3. Roll bread in parmesan cheese until evenly coated.
4. Cook on baking sheet, approximately two inches apart for about ten minutes or until brown. Let cool and serve.
5. Mix ranch dressing and pepper sauce until well blended. This is the dipping sauce for the bread bones. Add more pepper sauce if want a spicier dip or you can use a zesty spaghetti sauce or queso dip instead.

Swamp Dip

Ingredients (Serves 4 - 6):

- 3 avocados, peeled and cubed (can use frozen or premade guacamole)
- 2 tablespoons lime juice
- 1/2 teaspoon salt
- 1/8 teaspoon pepper
- 1/3 cup sour cream
- 1/4 teaspoon tabasco sauce
- 1 tomato, seeded and choppe d
- 4-6 cups green guacamole chips or blue tortilla chips

Directions:

1. Place avocado in medium bowl; add lime juice, salt, and pepper and mash using a potato masher to desired consistency. Stir in the sour cream, Tabasco sauce, and chopped tomato. Transfer to a serving bowl and surround with guacamole chips or dark blue or red tortilla chips.

2. Avocados contain healthy fats and are high in betasitosterol, which lowers bad cholesterol.

Pumpkin Pie Dip

Ingredients (makes 4 cups):

- 8 oz. cream cheese, softened
- 2 cups powdered sugar
- 1 1/4 cups canned pumpkin
- 1/2 cup sour cream
- 1/2 tsp cinnamo n
- 1/2 tsp nutmeg
- 1/2 tsp ginger
- 1/4 - 1/2 cup caramel sauce, store bought or homemade crackers

Directions:

1. In a large mixing bowl, blend cream cheese and powdered sugar until smooth and fluffy. Fold in pumpkin, sour cream, cinnamon, nutmeg, and ginger and mix until smooth and fluffy. Store in refrigerator in an airtight container until ready to serve. Drizzle with caramel sauce and serve with sweet crackers, such as graham crackers, chocolate wafers, or gingersnap cookies.

Halloween Popcorn Balls

Ingredients:

- 1 cup sugar
- ¾ cup margarine
- 1 ½ cups corn syrup
- ½ tsp. sal t
- 20 cups popped popcorn
- 4 cups candy corn (optional)
- Orange food coloring (yellow+red)

Directions:

1. Combine the sugar, margarine, corn syrup, and salt in pan over medium heat. Bring to a boil and stir for two minutes. Remove from heat. Add orange food coloring (enough to turn mixture bright orange and you can use other colors too if you want different colored popcorn balls, including green and purple (blue+red). Stir in popcorn and candy corn. Cool slightly (enough so that you can handle them but not so long as to make working with mixture impossible) and then begin shaping into balls about 4 or 5 inches in diameter. Cool on wax paper. Wrap balls individually in Halloween theme plastic wrap.

Tip: Dip hands in cold water before making balls.

Devils Snack Mix

Ingredients:

- 8 cups of rice, corn, & wheat cereal (or any combination thereof)
- 1 cup peanuts
- 1 cup mini cheese crackers (Nabisco Cheese Nips)
- 1 package taco seasoning (dry)
- 6 tbsp. margarine
- 1 tbsp. Worcestershire sauce
- 1 tsp hot pepper sauce (optional)

Directions:

1. Preheat oven to 250◦F. Melt margarine in roasting pan. Stir in taco seasoning, Worcestershire sauce, and hot pepper sauce. Then stir in rest of **Ingredients**. Bake for 1 hour, stirring every 10 – 15 minutes. Spread mixture on wax paper or paper towels to cool. Store in airtight container and then serve in Halloween theme bowl or canister or in individual Halloween cupcake holders.
2. TIP: There are lots of variations on this mix including using pecans, candy corn, cheese curls, and pretzels, depending on your preferences or what you have on hand. Or you can simply buy a bag of Chex Cereal Mix and empty into a bowl or individual cups or Halloween theme muffin liners! When I do this I add just a little seasoned salt and garlic salt as the store bought mix is a bit bland for my tastes.

Goblin Mix

Ingredients

- 1 bag or canister of mixed nuts
- 1 bag of candy corn
- 1 bag of Reese's pieces (optional)

Directions:

1. If you want something super easy and cheap but better than putting out a can of nuts, this is a good compromise .
2. Buy or mix together any combination of nuts you desire. Add a bag of Halloween them candy corn (mini pumpkins in Halloween colors). Toss and store in airtight container. Serve in Halloween theme cupcake holders or a large plastic Halloween bowl.
3. TIP: You can vary this recipe by substituting Halloween M & M's (I like pretzel M & M's in this recipe) or coconut flakes or whatever you like in lieu of candy corn. Or you can simply add a few chocolate covered peanuts or pretzel nuggets to mixed nuts.

Goblin Munch

Ingredients:

- 4 cups Golden Grahams cereal
- 2 cups Cocoa Puffs cereal
- 2 cups thin pretzel sticks
- 1 cup Reese's Pieces
- 1 cup dry-roasted peanuts
- 10 oz. white chocolate baking bars or squares, chopped
- 2 tablespoons butter or margarine
- ½ cup powdered suga r

Directions:

1. In large bowl, mix cereals, pretzels, peanut butter candies and peanuts; set aside.
2. In 1-quart microwavable bowl, microwave white chocolate and butter uncovered on High about 1 minute, stirring once, until melted and chocolate can be stirred smooth. Pour over cereal mixture, stirring until evenly coated.
3. In large food-storage plastic bag, toss half of the cereal mixture with 1/4 cup of the powdered sugar until evenly coated. Spread on waxed paper to cool. Repeat with remaining cereal mixture and remaining 1/4 cup powdered sugar. Store tightly covered at room temperature.
4. TIP: You can substitute whatever cereal, nuts, or candies you may prefer.

Sweet or tangy dip with vegetables

Ingredients:

- Mini pumpkin
- 12-16 ounces dip
- Raw veggies

Directions:

1. Make your own favorite dip recipe or use store bought dip. There are lots of great choices in the refrigerator section of most grocery stores, such as spinach dip and spicy southwest ranch .
2. Using a mini pumpkin, carve an opening at the top, gut it, and make sure the inside is clean and completely dry.
3. Transfer your bowl or container of dip into the cavity of the pumpkin. Serve with Halloween-colored veggies, such as celery sticks, green pepper strips, and baby carrots.
4. Tip: If you are pressed for time or simply don't want to clean out a pumpkin, you can buy a pumpkin plate/bowl at the dollar store (be sure to wash it) and use it for dip instead. But I do encourage you to buy a mini pumpkin and go for it. They only cost about $2 at most and are easy and fairly fast to prepare. Plus, I think the effect is worth the effort.

Halloween Seven-layer Dip (Individual Servings)

Ingredients:

- In order from bottom layer to top:
- Refried beans
- Guacamole
- Sour Cream
- Salsa (I like medium spicy but can use mild or hot)
- Shredded Cheddar or Mexican Cheese Blend
- Diced Tomatoes & Diced Green Onions (sprinkled on top)
- Diced Black Olives (optional)
- Tortilla chips (plain or tri-color)
- Disposable plastic drink cups

Directions:

1. This is great because there is no communal dip bowl or chip bowl. How much you buy of these Ingredients depends on how many people you want to feed. Also, these items are all available in cans, bottles, and plastic containers for convenience or you can make your own salsa or dice your own tomatoes if desired.
2. Put a few spoons of one ingredient into cup and smooth to create each layer. Start with the beans and then add the guacamole and then top with sour cream, etc.
3. Place chips along the sides of each cup on top of layers.
4. Cover each cup with plastic wrap if prepare in advance. You can make these tasty appetizers the day before (except for adding the chips) and keep in refrigerator until ready to serve. I like to buy bags of tri-color (dark blue, red, and plain) chips to use for this recipe.

Directions:

1. Preheat oven to 350°F.
2. In a large bowl, mix water, apple sauce, vanilla, egg, and honey with a whisk. Combine whole wheat flour and baking powder and fold into wet **Ingredients**. Add chopped apples.
3. Spoon mixture into greased muffin tins. I use mini muffin tins for smaller treats. Bake for 35 minutes; let cool.

www.ingramcontent.com/pod-product-compliance
Ingram Content Group UK Ltd.
Pitfield, Milton Keynes, MK11 3LW, UK
UKHW061705190726
13853UKWH00008B/2418

9 798456 506245